The Way of Jesus

Practising Resurrection in the Neighbourhood

Jay Thomas

"The Word became flesh and blood, and moved into the neighbourhood."
— John 1:14 (The Message)

BEFORE WE BEGIN

You don't need more content.
Not another five-step formula.
Not more noise dressed up as vision.
Or hype.
Or strategy sessions framed as sacred.

What if what you need— is less?
A pause. A breath long enough to remember.

Because something in you already knows:
The Church isn't what we've built.
It's what we've been, and what we could be again.

Not a brand to curate.
Not a programme to scale.
But a body—tender, messy, living.

A table where the chairs wobble
but the welcome holds.
A people who keep showing up.

Over the years, we've spent a lot of time drawing maps.

Doctrines. Systems. Models.
Trying to name the movement.

But the Spirit?
She doesn't stay where we've boxed her in.
She moves where feet touch soil.
Where grief lingers long after the meeting ends.
She's not on the paper.

She's in the faces on your street.
In the stories that don't make the newsletter.
In the rusted garden gate that still swings open.
In the child who knows your name
because you stayed.

This isn't a book of answers.
It's a book of invitations.

To walk slower.
To listen deeper.
To stop asking, *"What can we fix?"*—
and start asking, *"What's already alive?"*

Because the sacred was never meant to stay in the sanctuary.
It was always meant to move into the neighbourhood—
with flesh and dirt and laughter and grief.

And maybe your community doesn't need a visionary or hero.
Maybe it needs a witness.
Someone who sees what's already good
and says it out loud

Remember, you're not starting from nothing.

You're standing on ground already blessed.

This book isn't a call to reinvent the Church.
It's a call to remember her.

To look beneath the ashes,
the anxiety,
the attendance statistics—
and find the ember that still glows.

The Jesus-way has always been like that.
Quiet.
Relational.
Resilient.

A kingdom that grows in cracks,
in kitchens,
in the quiet of 3am phone calls
and the gift of a meal left at the door.

So bring your weariness.
Bring your questions.
Bring your ache for something real.

But most of all—
bring your neighbourhood.

Because resurrection doesn't happen at a distance.
It happens in the place where you live.
In the hands you already hold.
In the stories waiting to be noticed.

The Church isn't a machine to repair.
She's a people to re-member.

And the good news?
The Spirit is already ahead of you.

Hovering.
Beckoning.
Breathing.

So—
Let's begin.

INTRODUCTION

This is a book about the Church.
Not the Church we built to protect belief,
but the Church we're being called to become.

It's about what happens when the sacred spills out of
stained glass and into the streets.
When the body of Christ stops sitting still
and starts walking the neighbourhood again.

Somewhere along the way,
we mistook the map for the journey.
We built walls to hold what was meant to move.
And somewhere along the way,
we started calling that movement *"Sunday morning."*

But the story of God has always been bigger than a
single hour on a single day.

It's the story of a people.
Of presence.
Of going—not just gathering.

Somewhere deep in our bones,
we know:
the Church was never meant to be a bunker.
Or a brand.
Or a list of beliefs pinned to a website.

It was always meant to be a body.
Alive. Moving. Embedded in the everyday.

This isn't a call for innovation for its own sake.
This is a remembering.
A re-membering.
Putting the body back together.
Reattaching what's come loose—
from neighbours, from purpose, from pulse.

What if Church wasn't a place we go
or a service we attend,
but a way we show up—
as a people becoming love in the neighbourhood?

Because the Gospel isn't an abstract doctrine we defend.
It's a way of living we embody.
And Jesus didn't come to build an institution.
He came to inaugurate a kingdom—
a way of being in the world
that disrupts, heals, invites, and restores.

Look at the story.
Look at the rhythm.
From Israel's wilderness,
to the quiet places Jesus withdrew,
to the crowded spaces where he showed up,
to the courage of the early Church—

it echoes through time.

Isolation.
Then connection.
Then the ache—and gift—of sacrifice.
And the slow, surprising work of resurrection.

This book is an invitation to walk that rhythm.
To practice it with our lives.
To let it shape how we see the Church—
not as an event,
but as a way of being.
To let it transform how we show up in our neighbourhoods,
how we carry hope in our souls,
and how we become part of God's unfolding story in the everyday.

It rarely moves in straight lines.
It's not neat.
Not efficient.

But it's real.
It costs something.
And it's carried together.

This is how the Spirit moves.
Through silence.
Through story.
Through a people brave enough to stay at the table.

Exile and return. Solitude and solidarity.
Things fracture. And then—
grace begins to gather what's been scattered.

Not once.
Not as a formula.
But over and over.
Again.
And again.
And again..

In Acts, they wait behind locked doors.
Fearful. Unsure. Isolated.

Then the Spirit comes.
And they go.
Into the city.
Into the homes.
Into the mess.
No marketing strategy.
No polished programmes.
Just the power of presence.

And presence changes everything.

The Church doesn't start with a mission statement.
It starts with a meal.

With a conversation.
With people willing to show up.
Not with all the answers—
but with open hands and listening hearts.

So this isn't a manual.
There's no quick fixes.
But there is a compass.
And a way to walk.

To rediscover the sacred in the soil beneath our feet.
To listen again for the Spirit that's already at work in our communities.
To see the Church not as the hero of the story,
but as a humble participant in the healing of all things.

The Church isn't dying.
Maybe space is being cleared for something new to emerge
Trimmed back to its roots
so something more fruitful can grow.

So here's the invitation:

Step outside.
Look around.

Not for what you can build— but for who you can become.

It's deeper than launching the next big programme.
Maybe it's about the kind of community we're growing into.
Not just doing Church—
But becoming people of presence, of practice, and of purpose.

The kind of Church that moves at the pace of relationship?
The kind with soil under its nails,
and names spoken with tenderness,
like liturgy?

Could it be
that Church looks less like a sanctuary—
and more like a table,
right in the middle of the street?

The journey didn't end.
It just shifted direction.
And now—
it begins again.

And you?
You're invited.

Some Questions

What images or assumptions come to mind when you hear the word "church"?

How have you seen the Church become disconnected from its neighbourhood or community?

What do you think it means to "walk at the pace of relationship" in your context?

Where in your own life have you experienced God outside of a Sunday morning service?

What would it mean for you to become the Church, rather than simply attend it?

THE GIFT OF WILDERNESS

We know—
Isolation.
Not just as a word—
but as a weight.
A silence that echoes.
A space that stretches between us and them.
And sometimes, between who we are and who we were meant to be.

We treat it like a problem to fix.
A glitch in the system.
Something to rush through,
or push past.

But what if—
what if isolation isn't just absence?
What if it's also presence—
a different kind?
An invitation.
A slow unravelling that leads to something deeper.

Notice how Jesus' ministry begins.
He doesn't wander into the wilderness by accident.
He's led there.
By the Spirit.
And what's waiting for him?
Not comfort.
Not clarity.

But temptation,
and dust.
The kind of silence that forces you to meet yourself in the emptiness.

But—and here's the thing—
Jesus doesn't run.
Doesn't build a shelter.
Doesn't rush the process.
He stays.
He sits with the uncomfortable hush.

He meets the hunger.
And in the unspoken space,
something sharp is born.
Focus. Identity. Authority.

We often miss it,
because we're too busy trying to move on.
But in our haste,
we miss the forming that only quiet can do.

The desert, it turns out,
isn't empty.
It's full.

Of questions that strip us bare.
Of truths that stitch us back together.

The Israelites knew this terrain too.
Forty years in a dry place,
a holding pattern that felt like punishment,
but was really preparation.
Because God doesn't waste wilderness.
It's in the waiting that they were shaped.
Fed daily.
Taught to trust.

Formed not by what they had,
but by what they were given.

Isolation, in its truest form,
is not abandonment.
It's a calling.
To be found in what feels like being forgotten.
It's a sacred pause.
A reorientation.
A return.

To what?

To the core.
To the centre.
To the heartbeat beneath all our noise.
To what's left and what matters
when everything else is gone.

And maybe that's where we find ourselves now.
The Church—
not unlike the disciples, locked away,
waiting, watching,
unsure of what comes next.
Is this fear?
Or is it formation?

Is this loss?
Or is it learning? Because isolation isn't just a break in the action—
it *is* the action.
A pause with purpose.
A place to pay attention to the things we've been too busy to see.

It asks hard questions:

Who are we when the groups or projects stop running?
When the buildings go quiet?
When the systems no longer hold us up?

It asks:
What's inside us
when all the externals fade?

There are times when the most courageous thing a church can do
is stop.

Not because we've failed.
But because we need to listen.
Again.
And more intently.

Not every pause is a crisis.
They are opportunities and moments.
To breathe.
To notice.
To remember what is truly important
when the noise dies down.

What if we laid every programme down,
not to pick up something shinier,
but to find out what's actually needed now?

What if we stopped producing and creating more,
just long enough to become more present?

Stopped filling the calendar—
so the silence could speak?

Stopped solving problems—
so we could name the questions beneath them?

Stopping is not surrender.
It's stewardship.
Of the season we're in.
Of the people we've become.
Of the ground we've been given.

It's letting the soil lie fallow.
So it can breathe again.
So we can see again.
So we can be shaped
before we try to shape anything else.

And this, right here,
is where wisdom meets us—
because within every community,
there are seeds.
Stories.
Gifts.
People whose presence is a kind of prophecy.
But we'll only see them
if we are still enough to notice.

The wilderness is not barren.
It's just not familiar.
And that can feel like death.
But often, it's birth.

So maybe the question isn't
"How do we escape isolation?"
Maybe it's:
"What is this wilderness revealing?"

What resilience is rising?
What faith is being rewoven?
What capacities are surfacing that were buried by the noise?

And like Jesus,
we don't stay in the desert forever.
But we don't rush it either.
Because when we emerge—
and we will—
we come out different.

More grounded.
Less noise, more presence.
Less performance, more peace.
Less certainty, more compassion.

We come out not just as individuals,
but as reconnected communities.
Not with all the answers,
but with better questions.
Not with flashy solutions,
but with a deeper love.

So let us not waste this season.
Let it teach us.
Let it shape us.
Let it slow us down until we can hear again.

The Church that walks back out of the wilderness—
will not be the same Church that walked in.

But the wilderness—
it isn't just about what falls away.
It's about what begins to surface.
Not in grand visions or loud declarations,
but in the quiet clarity that comes
when there's nothing left to perform.

It's there, in the stillness,
that we begin to see again.
Not as consumers or leaders or problem-solvers—
but as neighbours.
As humans. As people who belong.

Because when the scaffolding comes down—
the systems,
the strategies,
the spotlight we've mistaken for the sun—
what's left is presence.

And presence, real presence,
is where love begins again.

We remember—
we were never meant to impress.
We were meant to be faithful.
To listen.
To linger.
To love without needing to control the outcome.

This is what the wilderness offers:
not clarity on command,
but a re-rooting.
Back to the ground we've been standing on all along.
Back to the stories already unfolding around us.
Back to the slow,
sacred rhythm of becoming.

Not a Church that rushes to be relevant—
but one that's willing to be real.

Because formation doesn't happen at scale.

It happens around fires.
On street corners.
In conversations that carry more silence than answers.

This isn't about leading our way out.
It's about noticing who we are becoming—right here.

Not after the silence ends.
Not when we've figured it all out.
But in the midst of it.

Because a Church that learns to stay in the wilderness long enough to listen—
will be a Church worth trusting when the silence breaks.

It will walk slower.
Kneel sooner.
Speak less—and listen more.
It will be leaner.
Kinder.
Braver.
And more attuned to the Spirit who has been with us
all along.

Some Questions

How have you experienced isolation in your spiritual journey? What did it reveal?

Can you recall a time when silence shaped you more than noise ever could?

What patterns or systems in your faith community feel like they need a wilderness season?

What are the "gifts" already present in your community that may have been overlooked?

In what ways might isolation be an invitation rather than a punishment?

WHERE LOVE WALKS

Eventually, the silence lifts.
The dust settles.
You step out of the wilderness—
not into comfort,
but into connection.
Jesus walks out of that wild space,
Not back to ease, but into encounter.
Into people. Into presence.
Into the aching, beautiful mess of being human.

He doesn't retreat to a mountaintop to shout truths into the void.
He walks straight into the everyday,
the markets and fishing docks,
into the crowds that push and pull,
to the people who don't belong anywhere else.
To the bruised, the sceptical, and the forgotten.

He doesn't just preach to them.
He eats with them.
He lingers.
He laughs.
He cries.

Because love doesn't just speak.
Love stays.
Love shows up.
Love gets close enough to touch.

Close enough to be felt.
And that's the shift—
from isolation to interaction.

This has always been the divine pattern.
It's the rhythm God's been tapping out since the beginning.
God doesn't outsource salvation.
God moves in.
Not above us.
Not around us.
But among us.

Incarnation is local.
It's specific.
It wears names.
It smells like fish and firewood.
It sounds like stories told late at night.

Jesus didn't come to build an institution.
He came to form a community.
And not a sanitised, polished one.
A gritty one.
Full of people with sharp edges
and painful stories
and unexpected gifts.

He touches lepers.
He listens to women with no standing.
He honours the faith of outsiders.
He tells stories about mustard seeds and unjust judges
and throws open the gates of the kingdom
to people who had been told they were on the outside.

This has always been the way God moves.
Even with the Israelites—

Desert people turned covenant people.
They were called not just to believe—but to belong.
To each other.
To the stranger.
To the land.

They were told:
Leave the edges of your field.
Welcome the sojourner.
Care for the orphan and the widow.
Bake generosity into the law.
Because once—you were the outsider.
So now, be the welcome.

Jesus picks up this ancient thread
and weaves it into a new kind of community.
A table with room.
A shared loaf.
A basin and towel.
And then—after the cross,
after death doesn't get the last word—
comes the moment that changes everything.

And notice where the Spirit lands at Pentecost.
Not on a temple.
Not on a throne.
But on a gathered group of people.
Ordinary people,
in-between people,
people still unsure of what's next.
And suddenly—
they can speak.
Languages they never practiced.

Because love,

always finds a way to be heard.

And now?
Now the Spirit still moves.
Not confined to cathedrals or clergy.
But in kitchens,
and community centres,
and street corners.
In the places the maps don't bother to name.
In the voices we've learned to ignore.

The church that learns to listen—
really listen—
will hear it.

So maybe the work isn't to ask people to come
but to go to where they already are.
To see not what's missing,
but what's already alive.

That cracked pavement where the kids kick a football around?
That's holy ground.
That woman who knows everyone's name on the estate?
She's already holding the community together.
That man fixing bikes in his shed for free?
He's running a liturgy of repair.

Love doesn't wait for permission.
It doesn't need a vision statement.
It listens first. It walks slow.
It learns the rhythm of the place
like you'd learn the beat of a song.

This is what Jesus did.
Not dropping in with answers—

but sitting long enough to understand the questions.

And maybe that's what we've forgotten.
That revelation doesn't always look like thunder or fire—
Sometimes it sounds like,
"How was your shift today?"
Or,
"Tell me what you love about this street."

Because the Spirit doesn't only speak in tongues.
She also speaks in raised beds planted together,
in borrowed tools and returned favours,
in shared cups of tea and long chats at the corner shop.

This is how the Church learns to breathe again.
Not by scaling up, but by rooting down.
Deep into the local,
and the lived.

Imagine it—
A Church that's less about impact,
and more about presence.
Less about numbers,
and more about being counted on.
A Church that doesn't build walls to keep itself safe,
but joins hands to keep others seen.

Because the Spirit doesn't just hover.
She inhabits.
Moves in.
And she speaks in the dialect of the everyday.
But you just have to stay long enough to hear it.

And when you do—
you'll start to see:
there's no such thing as a God-forsaken place.

Only places we've forgotten to bless with our attention.

The Church that stays curious—
that asks better questions—
that trades certainty for solidarity—
that's the Church people still believe in.

Not because it's perfect.
But because it's present.
And love, when it walks,
always leaves footprints of belonging behind.

But this means unlearning.
It means shifting from platform to presence.
From monologue to dialogue.
From spectators to participants.

It means shifting the focus.
From growth charts to missing voices.
From filling seats to finding those we've overlooked.

It's less about getting people in the room—
and more about showing up where life is already happening.

Because many churches have mastered the Sunday service
but have forgotten how to serve on a Monday afternoon.
They've built big stages
but forgotten how to set tables.
They say "*come*"
but Jesus keeps saying "*go.*"

And the neighbourhood?
It's not holding its breath,
waiting for rescue.
It's alive.
Teeming with sacredness.
Relationships.
Resilience.
Not in need of saving—
but in need of seeing.

So what's the real work of the Church?
Not more polished social media.
Not louder services.

But this:
Walk your street.
Learn the names.
Ask the better questions.

What do you care about here?
What do you love about this place?
What do you already have?

Because Jesus isn't confined to inside the sanctuary.
He's on the streets.
He's in the recovery group.
In the housing project.
At the night shift break room.
In the stories we dismiss.
In the hands we avoid.

We don't bring God to the neighbourhood.
We join the Spirit already at work there.

Because God has always been moving towards.
Towards the hurt.

Towards the left out.
Towards the overlooked.

And the Church?
It only finds its soul
when it moves that way too.

So—what if your church left the building?
Not metaphorically.
Not as a branding strategy.
But as a way of life.

Would it recognise Jesus in the faces it finds?
Would it know how to listen before speaking?
Would it come not to fix, but to be changed?

Because interaction—
real, embodied, sacred interaction—
will cost you control.
But it will give you connection.

And maybe that—
that brave, relational, Spirit-filled connection—
is what we've been longing for all along.

The question is no longer:
Is the Spirit moving?
The question is:
Are we?

Some Questions

Where in your neighbourhood or daily life are there "crowds" that Jesus would walk into?

Who are the people you tend to move away from that Jesus might move toward?

What does it mean for you or your church to shift from platform to presence?

How would your church change if you asked, "Who is missing?" rather than "How do we grow?"

What's one street, school, or space where your church could listen better?

A CHURCH THAT BLEEDS

There comes a point in every story
when something has to die.
Not because the story has failed,
but because it's growing.
Because some things—
even good things—
can't go with you
where you're meant to go.

The success and accolades.
The stage.
The perceived influence.
The need to impress.
To manage the image.
To keep the machinery humming,
even as it grinds down the soul.
At some point,
it all has to be laid down.
All of it.
Let go.
Crucified.

There's a dying that makes room for living.
And it starts with surrender.

Jesus doesn't just heal or preach or tell parables.
He walks straight into the fire.
He chooses the cross.

Not because he had to.
But because love walks all the way to the end.
And beyond.

This is the shape of the pattern.
Death.
Then life.

Surrender.
Then resurrection.
But the death always comes first.

The cross wasn't a detour.
It wasn't the tragedy in an otherwise hopeful story.
It was the story.
Jesus didn't just die *for* us.
He showed us *how* to die.
How to lose well.
How to lay it all down
and trust that what's real
can't be taken by death.

He could have avoided it.
Power was on the table.
Crowds in his corner.
He had momentum.
But he walked
past the cheering crowds
to the confrontation.
Past the temple gates
to the unjust trial.
Past every exit ramp
to the cross.

Why?

Because love doesn't play it safe.
Love absorbs the blow.
Love dismantles the illusion.
Love gives itself away.
Not because it's weak—
but because it is the fiercest force in the world.

And this is where the Church so often loses the plot.
We want resurrection
without death.
We want comfort
without cost.
We want influence
without letting go.
We want to carry the name of Jesus
but not the cross that comes with it.

But the invitation was never just to believe in the cross.
It was to carry one.

The early community knew this.
They didn't hedge their bets.
They shared what they had.
They emptied their pockets,
and sometimes their lives.
They refused to play along with the empire's script.
And they were formed by the same pattern.
Cruciform people.
Shaped by love that bleeds.

This rhythm isn't new.
It's been echoing through the story for centuries.
Think of exile.
Of Babylon.
The songs that went quiet.

The temple reduced to ash.
The people—dispersed, disoriented, and undone.

They wept.
They didn't fake joy.
They hung up their instruments.
But even in exile,
they learned to live.
To plant.
To build.
To raise their children in strange soil.
To seek peace in a place that once broke them.

Because exile isn't abandonment.
It's crucifixion.
It's the death of what we thought was permanent.
It's the burning away of what no longer gives life.

But if you stay long enough—
if you don't numb or flee or rebuild too fast—
you'll hear the prophets again.
You'll see what remains when the dust settles.
You'll find a remnant.
Not of buildings,
but of soul.

So maybe your church is in exile.
Maybe the crowd is gone.
The rhythm broken.
The building echoing with questions.
Maybe what worked
doesn't work anymore.

That might not be failure.
That might be grace.

Let it burn—
not in destruction,
but in refining.
Because resurrection isn't found
in getting back to normal.
It's found in letting the false die
so something deeper can rise.

Jesus dies outside the city.
Naked.
Rejected.
Bleeding between criminals.

That's God.
Not on a throne.
Not in the centre of power.
Not inside the sanctuary.
But on the margins.
In the sorrow.
With the forsaken.
With the forgotten.

If that's where God is found—
then maybe that's where we belong too.

A crucified church doesn't pretend.
It doesn't hide its bruises.
It doesn't dress up loss in polite language.
It doesn't perform.
It tells the truth.
It weeps.
It repents.
It listens.
It makes space.

Not because it's figured it all out,

but because it finally stopped trying to.

So maybe the church that embraces sacrifice
isn't bigger,
louder,
or flashier.
Maybe it's smaller—on purpose.
Slower—by conviction.
Less efficient, maybe,
but more faithful.

Less impressive to the world,
but more alive to the Spirit.
Because this church
no longer shapes itself around relevance,
but around resonance.
It's not trying to climb the ladder—
it's learning how to kneel.

It's not chasing metrics.
It's cultivating fruit.

Because it's no longer conformed
to the image of cultural success—
polished, marketable, scalable—
but formed in the shape of a cross,
and a tomb,
and a love that would rather be broken
than break others.

A love that would rather bleed
than brand.
A love that empties itself
so something sacred can take root.
And somehow, in that surrender,
it becomes a signpost to a different kind of world.

A world already breaking in.
Already here.
Hidden in plain sight.
At the margins.
In the dirt.
Where love always goes.

It's not about rebuilding what fell.
It's about recognising what's already growing—
quietly, steadily—
in the people around us.

Because the Church has never been just the steeple or the sermon.
It's the shared meal.
The lifted head.
The open hand.

Resurrection is not a return to status.
It's a return to soul.
To story.
To solidarity.

So what if resurrection looked like drawing near again?
To your neighbour.
To your community.
To the ones who thought they were forgotten?

What if the next chapter of the Church was not written in strategy documents—
but in shared laughter,
in walking the dog with someone who's grieving,
in pausing long enough to really listen?

Because God isn't waiting for us
to gather a crowd.

God is already here—
in the face across the table,
in the question no one's yet asked,
in the courage to begin again
And maybe the question isn't
"How do we bring them back?"
but
How do we be here, fully, with whoever's already come?"

This is the invitation.
Not to revive the glory days.
But to follow the Spirit
into what is being made new.

Some Questions

What illusions, systems, or habits are you being invited to let die?

How has your church tried to skip crucifixion and move straight to resurrection?

When has exile—in your faith or life—led to unexpected clarity or growth?

What fears keep your community from embracing the path of surrender?

What might it look like for your church to tell the truth about its wounds?

THE RISEN CHURCH

Something happened.
Something unthinkable.
Something holy.
They went to the tomb,
expecting finality.
Silence.
A sealed stone.
A still body.
But the grave had been interrupted.

There were angels.
There were whispers.
There were linen wrappings,
folded and left behind.

He's not here.

He's risen.

And just like that—
everything changes.

If death doesn't get the last word,
maybe despair doesn't either.
Maybe loss doesn't hold the power we gave it.
Maybe pain can speak— but not define.

Resurrection doesn't erase death.
It honours it.
It walks through it.
It carries the scars—
and still breathes.

Jesus didn't come back to how things were.
He came forward—
into what could be.

Alive.
More alive than ever.

And this—
this is the invitation.
Not to admire the resurrection.
Not to decorate it in lilies once a year.
But to live it.
To embody it.
To become it.

A resurrected community.

But let's be honest— sometimes we don't look very alive.
We carry our pasts like backpacks of stone.
We fear what we don't understand.
We let hope starve while old systems feast.
We call it tradition,
but it's more like avoidance.
We confuse safety with faithfulness.
We preserve the frame
but let the fire go out.

But the first followers—
they burned.
Tongues of flame,

languages they didn't know they could speak,
healings they never saw coming,
meals that fed more than just hunger.

The Spirit poured out,
and suddenly the old lines didn't hold.
Jew and Gentile.
Rich and poor.
Free and enslaved.
Male and female.
All in.
All one.

Not because they had better theology.
But because they knew—
he was alive.
Actually.
Physically.
Unstoppably.

So they lived like it.
Shared like it.
Welcomed like it.
Risked everything
because they had already died to what held them.

This wasn't a new idea.
It was the oldest one.
Buried deep in the bones of the story.

Remember Ezekiel and that valley?
All those bones.
Dry.
Dispersed.
Disconnected.

God asks,
"Can these bones live?"
Ezekiel doesn't know—but God does.

"Speak to the bones."

And he does.
And the bones rattle.
Sinews stretch.
Flesh wraps.
But there's no breath—
not yet.

So God says,
"Call the wind."

Then breath moves in,
and what was many becomes one.
A body.
An army.
A people.

Because resurrection isn't just personal.
It's communal.
It's for the collective.
For the broken family.
The scattered body.
The divided Church.

It's for churches split by politics.
For communities too tired to sing.
For pastors wondering if it's over.
It's for the ones still showing up,
even with nothing left to prove.

It's for *us*.
To remember who we are.
And who we belong to.

Resurrection always leads to re-connection.
Always moves toward restoration.

But what does resurrection look like on a Monday morning,
with washing to hang
and bills to pay?
What does it sound like when the prayers are dry,
the pews are half-empty,
and the street outside doesn't even notice
the bell tower anymore?

It might not look like victory.
Not the kind we were taught to expect.
It might look more like visiting a neighbour
who's not had company in weeks.
Or putting the kettle on
when someone's crying in your kitchen.
It might sound like the laughter
that comes after tears,
or the silence you hold
so someone else can speak.

Resurrection,
you see,
doesn't always arrive with trumpets.
Sometimes it walks with a limp.
Sometimes it speaks in stammers,
with a bruised kind of hope
that still dares to rise.

Because being raised

doesn't mean we float above the pain.
It means we stay present in it,
and choose love anyway.

This is not the age of Christian empires.
That door's closed now.
And maybe that's a mercy.
Because the Church was never meant to sit at the head table.
It was always meant to gather on the margins—
with the hungry,
the doubting,
the ones who've had enough of performance.

So what if resurrection isn't about getting bigger?
What if it's about getting closer?
To each other.
To the story.
To the street.

Because a resurrected people
aren't obsessed with preserving the institution.
They're devoted to sharing life.
Real life.
Life that forgives.
That listens.
That doesn't need to win the argument.
That lights a candle
even when the night feels thick with grief.

There's this ancient promise—
tucked into the scroll of Isaiah.

A whisper for weary people and worn-out places:
"Your people will rebuild the ancient ruins
and will raise up the age-old foundations;

*you will be called Repairer of Broken Walls,
Restorer of Streets with Dwellings."*

Not just poetry.
Not just a metaphor for a better time.
But a declaration.
Of what happens when a community awakens.
When the Church stops asking how to grow
and starts asking how to love.

Because those ancient ruins?
They're not just buildings.
They're relationships worn thin.
Dreams buried too early.
Communities gutted by disconnection.

And those foundations?
They're trust. They're tables.
They're gardens growing where asphalt once ruled.

A church that roots itself in its neighbourhood,
that listens more than it speaks,
that joins—not saves—
will be the one that rises.

Not above the world.
But within it.
Woven in.

The risen church isn't louder.
It's more present.
More grounded.
More human.

One wall mended.
One street restored.

One neighbour seen.
This is how resurrection walks down the road.
Not just to Emmaus,
but to your front gate.

You want to see the Spirit moving?
Don't look for the spotlight.
Look for the leftovers.
The ones everyone forgot to count.
That's where Jesus tends to show up.

He's still in gardens,
calling names.
Still on roads,
walking with the confused.
Still in upper rooms,
showing wounds and saying,
"*Peace.*"

And he's still breathing on people
who doubt they can go on.

So if you're tired—
you're in good company.
If you're unsure—
you're not alone.
If you're still turning up,
even after disappointment,
even with questions in your pocket—
then hear this:

You are part of the resurrection.
Not just a spectator,
but a participant.
A carrier of breath.
A bearer of good news that doesn't need a platform—

just a willingness to love.

So let's not wait
for everything to feel certain.
Let's not stall
until the branding's better
or the lighting's just right.

Let's start where we are.
With what we've got.
Because the Spirit is already here,
hovering over what looks like chaos,
whispering again the oldest truth:
This too can be made new.

So rise with it.
Move with it.
Be the breath that calls bones to life,
the hands that rebuild broken walls,
and the heart that welcomes the stranger.

Some Questions

What does it mean for you to live as though Jesus is truly alive?

Where have you seen resurrection in your life—not reversal, but transformation through pain?

Which "bones" in your community feel dry? What might it mean to speak to them?

How can your church foster unity across lines of difference and division?

What do you need to lay down so something new can rise?

THE JOURNEY STARTS AGAIN

What now, Church?
The stone has moved.
The wind has come.
Grave clothes lie folded in the quiet.

We are not called back into comfort,
but forward into risk.
Into streets.
Into stories.
Into the sacred mess of movement.

Because resurrection
was never meant to be the end.
It's a beginning.
A crack of light at the edge of everything familiar.
And like every beginning,
it asks for movement.

There's a rhythm here:

Retreat.
Return.
Fall.
Rise.
And then?
Walk.
Live.
Go.

Resurrection doesn't set up shop at the mouth of the grave.
It doesn't turn the tomb into a shrine.
It moves.
It walks.

Jesus met them on roads they didn't expect,
on shorelines where their nets came up empty,
in rooms bolted shut by fear.

He eats with them.
Speaks peace.
Points forward.
To Galilee.
To the ends of the earth.

This is how it works:
Faith isn't still.
It flows.
It presses onward.
It pulses through story and scar alike.
It is not something you possess.
It is something you walk.

Maybe you lead a community.
Or maybe you're holding faith by a thread.
Either way—hear this...
The road begins again.
Always.

Because the One we follow
does not wait at checkpoints.
He's ahead of us—
already sitting at the table of someone we forgot,
already breathing life into corners we thought were done.

He goes before.
And we are invited to follow.

And that journey—
it's never just about personal change.
It's about transformation with dirt under its nails.
It's about gardens planted in bomb craters.
Meals cooked in burned-out kitchens.
Fences pulled down plank by plank
to build longer tables.

This—
this is the Church.
Not an address.
Not a schedule.
Not a slogan.

But people.
Pilgrims.
The persistent ones.
The ones who love after betrayal.
Who show up after denial.
Who stay because love stays.

Remember Peter?
He failed with the volume turned up.
But resurrection didn't come with revenge.
It came with breakfast.
And a question:
Do you love me?

Then feed.
Then walk.

And walk he did.
Not for power.

Not for platform.
But for love.

Or the exiles—
those who returned to shattered walls and half-sung songs.
They wept as they laid stones.
They planted again,
even when the harvest felt far off.
They lifted their voices,
cracked though they were.

They trusted
that God wasn't done.

And they were right.

Because resurrection doesn't just happen in upper rooms.
It happens in ruins.
In deserts.
In the wreckage of yesterday's plans.
In the shaky courage of today's yes.

The Church isn't waiting on a better strategy.
She's waiting on people who know how to listen.
Who can spot life even while it's still underground.
Who recognise the sound of roots breaking soil.

Because not all resurrection is loud.
Sometimes it sounds like a kettle boiling in a quiet kitchen
where someone's finally being heard.
Sometimes it looks like a teenager stacking chairs
before they know the creed by heart.
Sometimes it feels like forgiveness—
not declared,

just offered.
In silence.
In a sigh.
In the sacred ordinary.

There's this myth
that the Church will one day become impressive.
Shiny.
Sorted.
But maybe that's the wrong dream.
Maybe she's meant to become more human.
More honest.
More like the Teacher
with dust on his feet and a towel in his hands.

So if you're standing in a hall
that smells of old coffee and last week's hope—
look again.
The Spirit doesn't need a stage.
She needs a people.
Willing to show up.
To become seed.
Small. Hidden.
But alive.

Resurrection doesn't compete with death.
It outlasts it.
Quietly.
Faithfully.
One conversation at a time.

So maybe it's time
to let go of the map.
To stop clutching the past
like a souvenir,
and stop fearing the future

like it's a threat.

This isn't only about tearing down what was.
It's about planting what could be.

Not just naming what's broken in the Church we inherited,
but becoming the soil for the Church we imagine—
together.

Where critique gives way to courage,
and every lament becomes compost for new life.

Because the Church we need won't fall from the sky.
It will rise from the ground. Maybe we start by asking:
Where is life already stirring around us?
And how do we join in?

This is the Church that could be.
Not the one we memorised.
But the one that's needed now.

A Church that listens before speaking.
That shows up without needing to fix.
That learns from the bruised.
That walks into tension
not to win—
but to love.

So, beloved community,
step out.
Wipe the dust off your feet.
Take courage.
The road is open.
Not behind you—
but beneath you.
In your breath.

In your bones.
In the stories waiting to unfold.

And the journey?
It starts again.

Some Questions

Where do you sense the Spirit inviting you to "walk" rather than wait?

What have you been holding onto—maps, expectations, strategies—that you need to release?

How can your community become a space of transformation "with dirt under its nails"?

What does faithful presence look like in your everyday rhythms?

What would it mean for your church to begin again—not with control, but with courage?

THE NEIGHBOURHOOD CHURCH

Resurrection isn't just a doctrine we affirm.
It's a life we embody.
More than creeds, more than Sundays—
it takes up space in the real world.

Resurrection needs skin.
It needs hands that hold.
Feet that go.
Faces that are not afraid to be seen.
It needs people who don't flinch at the mess.
People who sweat.
People who stay.
People who show up even when it's awkward.
Who trade comfort for presence.
Who choose proximity over perfection.

Because the goal was never just belief.
It was embodiment.

So what does a Resurrected Church look like—
not in theory,
but in practise?
In streets and stories.
In broken places.
In the middle of it all.

This doesn't mean discarding the past.

The Resurrected Church still gathers.
Still prays.
Still sings the old words—
but with new breath.

But then—
it moves.
From pews to pavements.
From prayers to presence.
From sanctuary to street.
Into the places where life is still deciding whether it's welcome.

It walks into schools,
hospitals,
community halls,
courtrooms,
town halls.

It kneels beside the lonely,
the laid-off,
the forgotten.

It shows up at the food bank—
not as saviour,
but as sibling. Because that's what love does.
It shows up.
Among us.
In the concrete and the questions.

The Church reborn doesn't preach from a distance.
It crouches beside the desk.
It learns names.
It sharpens pencils.
It reads with kids after the bell.
It says to teachers, *"We see you. We're with you."*

Because the child who forgot breakfast matters
just as much as the one who's never heard a Bible story.

It doesn't try to convert the classroom.
It commits to it.
Shows up.
Listens.
Lingers.

The Church that's risen knows how to sit in silence.
It doesn't rush to fix.
It doesn't need a tidy answer.
It creates room—real room—for honesty.

It trains ears, not just mouths.
It partners with professionals
not to replace—but to uphold.

And when someone says, *"I'm breaking,"*
it doesn't offer platitudes.
It says, *"You're not alone. Me too. Let's walk."*

It builds spaces where the soul can breathe again.

It opens its doors—
and then it opens its eyes.

It cooks meals, yes—
but it also asks why they're needed.
It questions systems.
Learns how policies shape poverty.
And then it speaks.
Loud enough to be heard.
Quiet enough to hear back.

It marches.

It writes.
It forgives debts.
It shares meals,
not to perform charity—
but to practise kinship.

This Church doesn't ask, *"How do we bring people in?"*
It wonders, *"How can we bless what's already blooming?"*

It does not come as expert.
It comes to learn.
To receive.
To be transformed by the ones it meets.

Because the Spirit was never waiting for us to show up—
She was already moving.

It sees gifts before needs.
It doesn't arrive with answers.
It arrives with curiosity. It offers its walls—
for artists, gardeners, dreamers, dancers.
For recovery circles.
For kids fixing broken bikes.

It doesn't compete.
It co-creates.
Because the Spirit—
didn't wait for the steeple to show up.

It doesn't retreat from screens.
It inhabits them—with grace.
With beauty.
With truth that breathes instead of barks.

It crafts liturgies that live in pockets.
Tells stories that kindle wonder.

It sees people, not just traffic.
Responds with love, not just likes.

The online world isn't fake.
It's real soil.
And resurrection can grow there too.

This Church gets its hands dirty.
Turns lawns into meadows.

Teaches compost like it's catechism.
It picks up trash like a sacrament.

It prays under trees.
Holds climate vigils.
Plants hope into hard ground.

Because creation isn't just a backdrop to the Gospel.
It's part of the story.
Part of the resurrection.
Not every church will do all of this.
And that's okay.

The point is not perfection.
It's participation.
Rooted.
Relational.
Real.

Because resurrection—
it's always local.

You might ask, *"What if we mess it up?"*

You will.

But grace isn't a parachute.
It's soil.
It's what you grow in.

And Jesus—
He's already walking ahead.
Breaking bread.
Waiting.
Not in shame.
But in joy.
In welcome.
In invitation.

So ask your neighbourhood,
"What do you need?"

Then ask your church,
"What do we have?"

And start there.

Not with a programme.
But with presence.

Because resurrection isn't abstract.
It has a face.
A name.
A need.
A neighbourhood.

And in the 21st Century,
resurrection might look like a mentoring hour.
Or a poetry night.
Or a mental health hub.
Or a protest.
Or a garden.

Or a kitchen.
Or a quiet room.
Or a long walk with someone who's grieving.

It might not shine through stained glass.
It might flicker on a street corner.
Or glow softly in a recovery group.

But it's real.
And it starts when we show up.
It starts not in theory,
but in touch.
In presence.
In place.

Some Questions

Where is your church physically present—but spiritually absent?

How can your church community bless what's already blooming rather than try to import something new?

What do you already have that could be shared with your neighbours?

What's one small, tangible way your church could embody resurrection this month?

What does it look like to "show up" not with solutions, but with presence?

THE PARABLE OF THE GARDEN GATE

There was once a village
with a garden at its heart.

No one knew who planted it.
Some said it had always been there.
Others whispered it began with a single seed—
buried by someone who wasn't looking for credit.

There were no fences.
No rota.
No grand opening.

Just soil,
and benches,
and food that grew without permission.

People wandered in.
Shared what they picked.
Sat in silence.
Laughed out loud.
Left scribbled prayers in the cracks of the wall.
It wasn't tidy.
But it was alive.
And somehow,
it belonged to everyone.

Then one day, a group gathered and said,
"This is holy ground. We should protect it."

So they built a gate.
Not to keep people out, they said—
just to know who was in.

They made a schedule.
Drew up rules.
Hung signs.
Tidy signs.
With phrases like:
"*Please respect the harvest.*"
and
"*Benches available during designated hours.*"

And in some ways, it worked.
The garden stayed neat.
The tools stayed clean.
The gate stayed shut.

But fewer people came.

The children stopped running through the marigolds.
The old man who used to whistle by the thyme
wasn't sure if he was still allowed.

One day, someone added a plaque to the gate:
Visitors welcome—by arrangement.

And that's when the weeds came.
Not because people were careless.
But because no one came at all.

Until—
a woman arrived.
She didn't ask.
She climbed the low wall at the back.
Found the old watering can in the shed.

And began.

Not with a plan.
Not with a sermon.
But with a spade.
And a quiet hello to anyone who passed.

She watered.
She weeded.
She hummed while she worked.
And slowly—
almost imperceptibly—
the gate rusted open again.

And the garden remembered
what it was for.

THE SPIRIT HOVERS

Hope doesn't shout.
It hums.
Low.
Steady.
Resilient.

It sings behind hospital curtains.
It stands in the rain at a march.
It lingers in quiet moments
when nothing feels certain—
yet the next breath still comes.

Hope isn't naiive.
It's not blind to pain.
It doesn't say, *"Everything will be fine."*
It says, *"Even if it's not—we will still build. Still plant. Still love."*

Because that's what Jesus did.
He showed up.
In the margins.
On the shoreline.
At tables where no one else would sit.
In the garden, when all hope seemed lost.

In a body.
Then a broken one.
Then a glorified one.

Still with scars.

And He never left.

This isn't a blueprint.
Or a strategy.
Or a five-step model for revival.

It's a vision.
A pulse.
A remembering.

That the Church is most alive
not when it's performing—
but when it's participating.
When its hands are dirty.
When its heart is open.
When its doors are wide.

I see a Church that lives by breath.
By rhythm.
By retreat and return.
By silence and song.
By giving and receiving.
By dying and rising.

A Church that listens first.
That welcomes without conditions.
That weeps without rushing to fix.
That sees Jesus
in the worn face of a father who can't pay rent,
in the addict who keeps trying,
in the teen who can't stop panicking.

And yes, it leaves the building—
not because buildings are bad,

but because the world needs something more than walls.

It needs presence.
Light.
Bread.
A story worth living.

It needs you.

So here's your vision of hope:
The same Spirit who hovered over chaos,
hovers still.
Brooding.
Breathing.
Calling.

The question isn't *"Where is God?"*
It's *"Will we go with Him?"*

Because resurrection isn't just an event.
It's a direction.
A doorway.
A rhythm.
A road with dust and wonder on it.
And it's already begun.

Some Questions

What does hope mean to you—not optimism, but resilient faith?

Where have you seen quiet, defiant hope rise in hard places?

How do you experience the rhythm of withdrawal and return in your life?

What does it mean to you that resurrection is not an event, but a direction?

What is one area where you feel God saying, "Will you join me?"

A RULE OF RESURRECTION

Living the Way of Jesus Together
This isn't a checklist.
It's not a programme.
It's not about getting it right.

It's a rhythm.
A posture.
A way of being in the world—
with one another,
with the wounded,
with the Spirit who still hovers over the deep.

We don't follow it to prove anything.
We follow it so we don't forget.
Who we are.
Whose we are.
What this is all for.

DAILY — Be Present

Before we change the world, we learn to see it.

Begin with breath.
One deep inhale. One slow exhale.
No rush. Just presence.
Whisper, "Here I am."

Notice one thing.
A neighbour. A bird. A broken pavement
Let it speak.
Let it interrupt the blur.

Practise one act of mercy.
A text. A smile. A silence held.
Don't wait for something big.
Resurrection often begins unnoticed.

WEEKLY — Hold Rhythm

Jesus walked roads. He didn't build monuments. He shared meals, not models.

Share a table.
No agenda.
Just food.
And faces.
And time.

Withdraw for a while.
Put down the noise.
Walk.
Light a candle.
Let the silence name what words can't.

Show up somewhere unexpected.
Not to fix.
But to stand alongside.
In the waiting room.
At the shelter.
In the school corridor.

MONTHLY — Live Together

The Church was never a building. It was always a body.

Ask the neighbourhood,
"What do you love about this place?"
"What do you need?"
Listen like you mean it.
No clipboard.
No hidden plan.

Offer what you already have.
A room.
A garden.
A gift.
A Story.

Hold space for lament.
Gather.
Light a candle.
Name what's been lost.
Let the tears fall.
God hears them all.

Seasonally

The tomb is empty, but the journey is just beginning.

Name the resurrection stories.
Tell them around firepits.
At potlucks.
In newsletters and late-night phone calls.
Not polished.
Just real.

Return to the rhythm.
Not with guilt.
But with grace.
This is not about perfection.
It's about staying in the flow.
Staying in the Way.

Bless the next mile.
Speak peace over the road ahead.
Over your community.
Over the world.
Over yourself.

POSTURE — Grace Over Grind

You'll miss a day.
Forget a month.
Grow weary.
It's okay.

This isn't about mastery.
It's about memory.
About remembering who you are—
and whose breath is in your lungs.

Because grace is not the fallback plan.
It's the soil.
The place we grow from.

What to Call It?

You might name it:

The Way of Resurrection
A Rhythm for the Road
Practicing Presence, Together

Call it whatever helps you remember this:

Resurrection isn't a holiday.
It's not a doctrine to defend.
It's a life to live. On your street.
At your table.
In the middle of everything that still feels unfinished.

A SENDING FOR THE ROAD AHEAD

Go now—
not with answers,
but with eyes open.

Not carrying plans,
but noticing people.

Trade the blueprint
for a bench.
The vision statement
for a shared loaf.
The platform
for a porch.

May you plant—
not programmes,
but presence.

May you speak less to impress,
and more to understand.

May your questions come slower,
and your listening grow deeper.
May your church
lose the need to shine—
and learn how to stay.

Not a monument to preserve,
but a table to expand.
Not a brand to market,
but a story to join.

And when you don't know what to do—
walk the street.
Name what's good.
Bless what's already growing.
And begin again.

With dirt under your nails.
And love in your bones.

Printed in Dunstable, United Kingdom